THE TRIGGER WARNINGS OF

CARAMELIZED BUTTERFLIES

WRITTEN AND ILLUSTRATED BY

AYANNA JADE LUEVANO

dedication

to all the women before and after me who struggled
through their adolescence, suffered with their
dependence, experienced bouts of dysmorphia, were
driven to sheer madness, felt the wrath of violence,
or fell madly in love;

may you fall in love with being alive.

trigger warning

this book contains topics including eating disorders, body dysmorphia, mental illness, suicide, self-harm, addiction, loss, domestic abuse, and infidelity.

read at your own discretion.
consuming this may be a hard pill to swallow.

this book isn't meant to be inspirational. this book is my way of getting my deepest, toughest thoughts out of my head and onto paper. i would lie and say, 'it gets better,' but i don't know that to be true *yet*; what i can say is that i am being honest.

the trigger warnings of

caramelized butterflies

ayanna jade luevano

the trigger warnings of

caramelized butterflies

prologue

poetry is corny

poetry is to be taken as seriously as you let it

poetry is deep

poetry is satirical delusions

poetry is a souped-up string of pretty words that

make you feel something

poetry is cringe

poetry is the crisp air in my lungs released as warm

sighs of relief that someone finally put into words

what you've been feeling your whole life

poetry is humbling

poetry is i

and you are poetry

how arrogant

poetry is that hopeless romantic who continues

reading and romanticizing despite it all

and that's why you're here

despite the post-sex-clarity feeling after reading,

you'll still feel the tingling of my trials and

tribulations put into pretty words,

and that made you feel something.

so let live and let poetry.

adolescence

i want you to be happy
i want that for you
please just be happy

i hope one day we can look back on this
and come to terms with who we are,
and what we're doing

bucket listed
-september 9th, 2021

adolescence

from sugar rushes to boy band crushes

waited ages to have a friend

from middle school dread to lips painted red

from crushing pills to kitchen counter bills

i just want to be myself again

i mourned this day before it came

i knew life would never be the same

spent too much time worrying

never enjoying the moment

god, i don't even know where home is

homeless
-november 11th, 2022

i've been thinking too hard about my book now that i'm reading it through people's eyes and getting self conscious

Don't think like that. It's art. It's yours.

Take it or leave it

through your eyes
-august 10th, 2024

teary eyes gleaming

in the main light of my small town

these lights know so many secrets

these lights glared down on my growth

red light

-september 12th, 2022

this town is burning

a simulation of hell

this town is only made to kiss and tell

this town is spirit-infested

liquor stores and ghosts on every corner

but this town is a masterpiece

after all, it brought you to me

town square festivals of laughter

cattle drives and pastures

stomping grounds for the weak

little ladies, oh, the pills they seek

early morning lake sunrises

and friday night neon bar lights

sweet tea kisses and bar fight stitches

caramelized butterflies

magnetic forces held in eyes

this town is a hallmark postcard

people come to florida for margaritas on the beach

not with this town

all we know is beer, boats, blow, bars, brahmans

this town will have you on your guard

this town built me up to be a soldier,

it wasn't chosen; it was the draft

this town is something you're supposed to leave in

the past

and when everything is said and done

this town will end in ash

okeechobee, florida

-november 4th, 2022

so the rumor goes,

you will heal me

but all you did was steal

fucking thief

as i grow older

i feel pain in my shoulders from holding the weight
of your hurt

my youth is looking farther from my grasp

stretching my frigid limbs, begging for a halt

arthritis will build in my hands

as yours will continue spinning

you can't get any further away before you start
coming back

i beg for your forgiveness

and even if you feel the constant state of regret and
anxiety

you will always grow

no matter my repent, no matter my promises

forever seems like too short

but knowing you,

you will catch up to it eventually

even if you're running in circles

chronos

-august 5th, 2021

chasing to the edge of the fucking violence

did i mean to cause this much pain?

i should've known better

after all,

my parents are a testament to the lesson

i so graciously put off studying for

monkey see, monkey do

-may 2nd, 2024

i wonder all through the night,

if you had not been my first heartbreak,

would i not dread the thought of

walking down the aisle?

would i be eager to have a child?

would i hold your hand till your last breath

and take care of the funeral plans?

would i not have taken my mother's footsteps

and found you in another man?

questions for my father

i am a reflection of

turbulence and passion,

despair and laughter,

chaos with moments of calm,

calamity with a brief touch of hope.

i am an all-encompassing human form of my
parents' love.

all-encompassing

the thing about loving both girls and boys is

in every girl, i'll heal my inner child

finding someone opposite to my mother

in every boy, i'll hurt my inner child

finding a reflection of my father

bi-panic

at my age,

my grandmother was taking a six year old with her

to softball practice

my mother was changing a one year old's diaper

and i am mourning the loss of my baby

21

so what if i am a crybaby?

what is really wrong with that?

i am 8 years old

just don't listen to me

i won't bore you with the details

of me burdened my entire life with an

existential crisis

childhood mid-life crisis

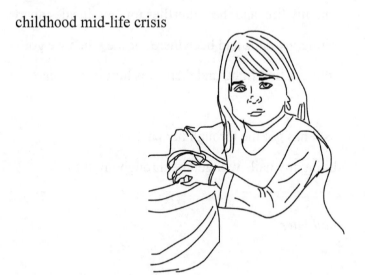

biting my nails is the truest constant in my life

how does one give that up?

biting my nails has been there for me

in my most vulnerable moments

biting my nails has been there for me

in my most anxious moments

biting my nails got me through my parent's divorce

biting my nails got me through high school

biting my nails was there for me when you came

into my life, and the butterflies tore my insides apart

biting my nails had been there for me when we got

into our first fight, and there was hurt in my heart

as it has got me through my past,

biting my nails will get me through my future

nail biter

be nice to your mom
it's her first time at life, too
it's her first time being her age
with a child your age
as you grow, so does she
she had a different life before you
you will have a different life after her
this period together is all you'll have
she lives a second life
experienced through your eyes
savor this adolescence
as it is your first time experiencing it,
it's also her last

growing pains
-august 4th, 2024

you taught me that leaving and starting over is the
bravest thing you could do
you taught me how to search for the ripest
strawberries in the winter
you taught me resilience through hardship
you taught me how to roll chicken and dumplin's
you taught me how to nurture the
marigolds and birds of paradise
you taught me how to drive,
admittedly, i'm still rusty
you taught me how the the leaves fall
you taught me how to nurse new growth
i may have been thick as thieves with my head,
but i remember the lessons for the day i decided to
learn

momma

a woman is staring at me

with eye contact

she's copying my every move

sometimes she's brushing her teeth

sometimes she's putting on lipstick

it scares me sometimes that she grew so fast

i remember her when she was just a little girl

with pigtails and a goofy smile

i wish she could've stayed that young forever

eye contact

heart of a child

mind of an adult

but a back that has carried the burden of girlhood

getting my strength back

the little girl you have disappointed through all
these years would just be happy you're alive,
fighting

you're okay
-july 23th, 2022

be the woman you needed
when you were a little girl
she would be ecstatic to know
you can stay up late
eat as much candy as you please
drive anywhere

as much as you feel lost,
she'd think you are the coolest
complete your inner child's dreams
be nice to yourself
you are her

inner-child
-august 4th, 2021

adolescence

adolescence

dependence

with a depleted faith, a powdered temptress calls
upon my given name with promises of an
ecstasy-ridden cloud i shall lay my skin and bones
upon
with further observation, i don't suppose i'll be
eager to return home soon
my farewell may be forever
given all goes wrong
compliments to the temptress, i suppose

blow kisses

the term

'getting rid of'

is just too much to handle within itself

the hoarder

-april 22nd, 2021

all you ever do is use, abuse, and crush me

just lay down

you know you can rely on me to give you warmth

no doubt i make you feel like you're floating

goosebumps always cascade over your skin

as i caress your freckle-filled cheeks

as we're kissing

i'll make you want more

blow your mind like a whore

my flushed round face

you'll never forget my silhouette

the sound of my name triggers something in you

baby, i can see it

i know you love me

that's why you're loyal to this feeling

more, more, more

i know it makes you sick when i can't get to you

in time on a rainy day

don't worry, i feel the same too

i'm the go-to when you're feeling blue

i know it's bittersweet sometimes

sniff the flowers

just give it a minute

oxycodone 10mg

-may 7th, 2021

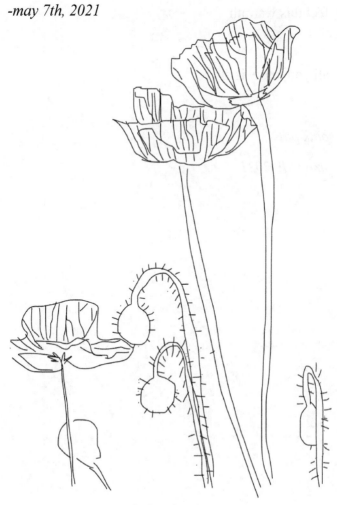

crush my ego

break me down limb by limb

line me up with your path of chaos

breathe in the smell of my hair

feel this warmth

all you know is sin

pink pill

-may7th, 2021

come down with me

then

cum down for me

dopamine depleted

dear honey,

i know things have changed

you no longer dance in your lingerie

things are so strangely different

now, even the medicine isn't the same

stop numbing your face

body shutters and the bitter taste

so tired of diminishing your grace

shaky hands, bloodshot doe eyes

banshee screeching mind

only quieted by a mild high

old highs, new lows

this corpse of a person is inside,

still fighting for me

my broken little heart

i kick it down every time it tries

i don't care if i'm dying,

i just want to get high

it'll all be okay if i get my fix

bandaid on a bullet hole

sitting on the floor, staring at the clock

back of my throat burning from absolute

death was my worst fear at fifteen

i was out at night snorting up every damn thing

now i have panic attacks for what's to come

i'm writing letters with mascara tears addressed to
the gun

things were easier when i'd snort a pill

that's the truth no one has the guts to tell

now i'm not the pretty little thing i was,

they say i look healthy, but i dread every crumb

i may not come down anymore, but nonetheless, i
feel worse

it does not get better

dependence

everyone says i look happy and healthy now

because i

gained weight

cleared my skin

grew out my hair

went to therapy

but i have never been worse

i long for the days i laid in bed

and felt the euphoria run through my body like silk

a tear used to fall down my cheeks when i'd

remember the feeling wasn't forever

and i dreaded the day i'd be here

i know this version of me makes everyone happy

but what about me?

i'm not happy

i just want to be in bed and feel good

it's the only time i felt a sliver of happiness

where is my serenity?

dysmorphia

dysmorphia

and like clockwork,

i stop putting food in my body

and thrive off the grumbling of my stomach

i am starving

dysmorphia

eating my feelings

then throwing up

flush that shame away

this is the key to survival

the battle of bulimia

-november 25th, 2019

i promise you i won't eat again

ever again

i love you, and i want you to like your body

i want you to be thin and beautiful

i promise i won't ruin that again

i promise i will be considerate of you

and your feelings

i will not put food in my mouth

if i do, stop me

don't let myself give in

i rather you starve if it meant confidence

don't let me say i don't care because you know i do

i will care later

please, i want you to be thin and happy

the ballad of the wretched eating disorder

-september 13th, 2021

wishing i would take up less space

in this bed right now

suck in, little angel

they can't see too much skin

what the fuck? why can't i do this?

my silhouette is something i wish i would've never

seen

why the fuck can't i be skinny?

skinny
-july 2nd, 2021

life is all about survival and reproduction
animals will do anything to
find their next meal and mate
they don't care about their reflection
it's ironic how humans will purposely not eat
for fear of how their reflection will look
and ultimately, that fear will be the demise of their
reproductive system

when did it all go wrong?

priorities

sickness was a flattering malady

so when you ask me if i lost weight,

i will say,

"why thank you, yes i did"

i know i was a big kid, but i'm older now

i may be grown, but i'm smaller

i'm not the tallest

but i will go to lengths you don't

understand to please the world

i might rupture earthquakes inside me

but i am beautiful now that i am sick

sickness

they tell you while you're young

beauty comes from the inside

so i drank a tube of lip gloss

and waited at the mirror

but i noticed too much

i picked at my face some

yelled at myself to control

and waited at the mirror

she told me i needed more

so i ate sparkly eyeshadow

noticed my tummy growing

and waited at the mirror

i snorted my setting powder

and took a swig of perfume

alcohol fogging my reflection

and i hated at the mirror

beauty is pain

but beauty will fill the void

beauty will become me

and i will become her

so i waited in the mirror

still waiting

-november 12th, 2022

you

you're so beautiful
but all i think is
why can't that be me?

letters to my past self
-july 2nd, 2021

dissatisfaction will be the death of me

i have got to stop romanticizing everything

skin and bones can't be accomplished

being as small as a child isn't realistic

i just want to be a kid again

never enough

-september 14th, 2022

the shine enhances the splatter of insecurity
on the only thing that i'm able to enjoy

delphiniums and cinnamon from the fake jewels i
decorate where music dances in the tunnels

the entrance to the speakers, where you will hear
my father's generational rage escape from

niagra falls is rushing out the windows of the soul

combing through the thick, coconut-vanilla-scented
forest filled with paths of dead ends

faces

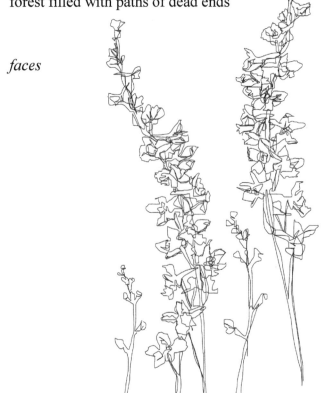

sometimes, it's the niche insecurities
that weigh on me the most

the vertical belly buttons
the narrow feet
the prominent collarbones
the long fingers
the small rib cage
the blonde arm hair
the legs that carry no scars
the small boobs

some things aren't attainable
and that's the slow burn of acceptance
i cannot bear

niche insecurities

when i looked at you in the cop car window
reflection, i cried

'cause, baby, i knew how scared you were

when i looked at you in the psych ward bathroom
mirror, i cried

'cause, baby, i knew how damaged you were

when i looked at you in the camera, i cried

'cause, baby, i knew how much you hated yourself

i know you hate what you see

i know you're sad for her

she's not getting better,

and when i see you in memories, i still cry

'cause i know how scared we are for us

how much longer can i look at myself?

i don't know this time

i cried

-november 13th, 2022

mascara running down my cheeks

staring at my reflection

feeling sorry for her

look into the mirror!

don't wince!

exposure therapy

-october 8th, 2022

you are a worthwhile person.

affirmation
-september 7th, 2022

dysmorphia

dysmorphia

madness

my therapist once said

i love things so intensely, and depending on how
i'm feeling at that moment, it's either the best thing
in the world or a grave problem.

being borderline has its charms and tragedies.

my favorite person can vouch for me;

they would say they've been someone i want such
intense close touch with. i'd even be willing to cut
into their body, step inside, zip it back up, and feel.

i just love things so intensely and depending on how
i'm feeling at the moment, it's either the best thing
in the world or a grave problem.

would i kill them at the expense of me loving things
too intensely?

or would i kill them for the satisfaction of hating
things too intensely?

my feelings are an overachiever in every sense

i am losing my mind

defective basket case

-april 24th, 2024

the light is gone from me

i am someone who i hate so much

all i do is bitch and moan and cry

i feel as if no one can stand to be around me

the truth is

i can't stand to be around me either

my sadness is a problem

i used to feel that everyone around me was

sucking the energy and life out of me

but i fear it is me who is the black hole

sucking the energy out of everything i can

and i can't stop

i am a tornado ruining everything in its path

sometimes i don't want to stop being the tornado

black hole

this will never be fair

i am in a constant tug-of-war with myself

the sad news is,

i am my own worst enemy

as i am the one who makes me cry

but the good news is,

i am the one who wipes my tears

i tuck myself in on the nights i cry myself to sleep

a constant abusive relationship with myself

manipulation in full effect

that's top-tier toxicity if you ask me

i wonder if i am no worse than you are to me

tug-of-war

-april 13th, 2024

i make myself get in the shower and sing.
singing makes my heart and soul feel warm.
when i sing, i can tell myself i'm okay.
it grounds me.

i'm told i need to learn to love myself. how? my
god, i've never known anything but deep hatred and
resentment for my entire being.

my soul? she's hurting and a crybaby, but she means
well. she's just in a constant state of unhappiness
and doesn't know how to improve. she has had all
the resources for years, learned coping mechanisms,
and practiced numeral tactics her whole life. in
some way, she's unfixable. she's damaged goods.
she wants to give up constantly because she feels
she'll never get better and doesn't care to. if getting
better means getting through right now, it's not
worth it. whether she plays the victim or is a victim,
it doesn't matter. it all comes down to the
never-ending agony of her mind.

some people want to watch the world burn;
others want to burn themselves.

coping skills undetected

using the butterfly wings to pull together

the gash on my thigh

damn, that's poetry within itself

note to self: self-harm is not poetry

-april 9th, 2024

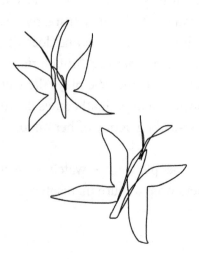

scarred limbs, warm shower floor

tangled hair, longing stares

doe eyes burning, my world kept turning

but i'm still yearning for ignorance

wondering like a child how to keep going

ambivalent to it all

ignorance is bliss

-november 6th, 2022

angels are crying all around,

but this isn't california

lost angels

-february 27th, 2022

i never noticed

how much i hated silence

i never noticed

how much i loved silence

anxious mess

-july 20th, 2022

sometimes
i look at you and
my mind fights
my heart flights
my eyes freeze
my mouth fawns

4f

i am a bomb

just waiting to explode

the times are ticking again

everywhere i look, there's a crater in sight

i look around, and disasters everywhere

don't know when the troops will retreat

but i am chained to the battlefield

hurting myself

i break my own peace treaties

feeling the fallout all alone

ashes to ashes

nuclear winter is taking over

i have not witnessed sunlight in ages

bomb

-march 15th, 2023

oceans are hidden in my seashells

the tsunamis,

      hurricanes,

           riptides,

                tropical storms

rattle inside

dreaming of crashing out and breaking free

if you listen closely, you can hear the water

yearning for escape

psychotic break

madness

i sleep with candles burning to see if

the flames will eat me alive in slumber

i feel lonely now watching the stars every night

i don't think i'll ever be free of the mourning phase

does forever reign true?

i'm not sure i know how to grieve for that long

left here to worry about your comfort

childhood movies messed me up

promising dreams come true

housefire

how can you enjoy something when i'm in a crisis?

how dare you enjoy something when i'm in a crisis

how do you enjoy something?

how are you not in a crisis?

i am, and you seem to enjoy it

crisis mode

-february 16th, 2024

i carry my spite for protection

necessary for survival and the first step to self-aid

ironically, it will not help either of us

 it is a double-ended knife

when hurt, i will wield the blade to stab you

even if my palms are split open in the process

don't worry! i will grab my butterflies

and pull my skin together again

if my pain is the cost of yours,

i will heal in my spite

i will carry that scar if it means we match

the state of grace period is a myth

i have my pain measured to a science;

my skin will grow together again

as it is not permanent

proper revenge is something infinite and irreversible

a true chemical change

i know my scar will never phase you, my death will

spite

a crime of passion may be the end all be all
all because i can't stop picturing you two
this is your doing; this is my gift to you
'cause the devils got horns, and so does the bull
you know these stomping grounds raised me
and i'm no longer playing the fool

so i read between the lines carefully
dissecting the cut
i adjust my trigger finger as well as
wield this blade with the wrath of female rage
ready to castrate, prepared for your fate
i suggest you steer clear of the road
with my footprints all over the scene
i'll shoot my whisky along with you under the bar
light gleam
daring you to be cruel and mean

my grandfather always said
there's no greater rush than hitting your target
and, darlin', you brought a knife to a gunfight

but my bullet comes with love bites
so beware, when passion consumes the crime
i always hit bullseye

bullseye

help!

i'm still here

when can i go?

i'm still waiting

-may 1st, 2022

they keep repeating, "life is hard"

so i destroyed this house of cards

boredom cascades the dominos

butterflies return to awaited cocoons

tsunamis filling my lungs

suddenly, i'm speaking in tongues

ophelia's voice calls upon me

my head is nearing its ease

the end

-october 24th, 2022

ophelia

delphiniums rooted in your fingertips

if only you knew that it was beautiful

if only you fell in love with being alive

secretly, my insides pulse for reasons you never did

only giving me the strength to follow your steps

jealousy precedes me

inhaling blue was not too much for you

but breathing was a task you could not accept

why do you suppose grazing fingers down your
throat was pure bliss?

your mouth opened wide for oceans

the concept of matter sent shivers down your spine,
i never blamed you for that

endlessly indebted to others' time

putting others in front no longer

oh, my dear, ophelia

your admirer is not far away

closer than you'd expect, never planned to stay

incessantly a muse struck with afflatus

dreaming of you under ricocheted moonlight

watching it shimmering on the water that held you
in its arms

longing to be embraced and feel safe

oh, my dear, ophelia

admiration suffocates me just breathing in your
presence

envy is a sin i cannot part with for you

following in your footsteps

the anticipation will fill my lungs as deep as the
seven seas

my dream, my long-awaited lover, my paramour

i'd say i love you more than life,

but isn't that the point?

ophelia

-april 2021

life never got tired of beating me

until death arrived

embraced my body

and said,

'warrior, be at peace'

that's what i've been waiting for all my life

memento mori

-september 2nd, 2022

to whom it may concern,
i wish to declare that my willpower has been given
over and is out of my control from this point
forward.

thank you!

emails to the universe

madness

violence

and i heard from the grapevine

you're one toxic motherfucker

doesn't matter

all i knew was i loved ya

rumors spread and spoiled every crop

you're poisoning everything you touch

doesn't matter

all i knew was i loved ya

vineyard

i want the taste of heaven

on my tongue,

not the burn of tequila

down my throat

the taste of you

-march 8th, 2022

something to nurture,

not something to conquer

be nice to me

-march 5th, 2022

my body uses her biological makeup

to cover the bruises you left

she's a talented artist

given she took the colourful hues away

although she can't remember

she'll never forget

the body keeps the score

cigars and patron on the beach

you smiled at me in approval

it was a blue haze fever dream

music vibrating in my heart

we're drunk in the palm trees

laughing like a child

with a death grip on the keys

lets go, i'd follow you anywhere

you make hell feel like a neon summer

you make living exciting

bring me down to my knees

false god, i pray for your laughter

ribs tired, giggling through the rapture

blue and brown eyes, bad lies, sunset skies

remind me of the love we have

tumbling waves and shaved ice

concrete hearts, the cracks fleshly repaved

sandy toes, and so the rumor goes...

you did the same with her

so why do i still feel special?

smiles turned to tears

how could you give truth to all of my fears

i need a drink right about now

what the fuck am i doing, babe?

devil's not too far away from reach

even after all you preach

i'd still look to you for mercy

begging, please, take me in your arms

no matter that you caused me this harm

i'll hide the black and blue you put on my eyes

neon summer

-november 14th, 2022

wish i had listened to all i heard

lightbulbs went off when you locked the door

you dragged my somber body across that hotel
room floor

how could you take the light away from me that
summer night?

june went into an ice age like you'd never believe

an unconditional love i'd never know to grieve

you tortured me senseless, i kicked and screamed

until the life growing inside was taken from me

i am frozen in orlando, florida

ice age

-november 5th, 2022

you said i looked prettier while i was sleeping

i think you just liked me when i was weak

vulnerable

-november 25th, 2022

i'm sorry you fell for a boy

and he made you sad

i'm sorry you still mourn your baby

the one you wish you still had

i'm sorry, miss

why do you have to make me feel small

so you can feel whole inside?

am i too much?

are you too small?

size comparison

-october 16th, 2022

it's icebergs kicked under the refrigerator

it's the rocky mountains swept under the rug

it's you pretending that you could ever actually love

me enough

i feel pathetic more often than i'd like to admit

elephant in the room

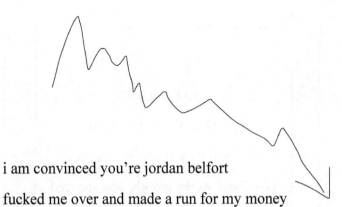

i am convinced you're jordan belfort

fucked me over and made a run for my money

left me with nothing but crisis

plummeted

-march 22nd, 2022

you're a liar

you lie, it's what you do

it's the only job you've ever had

somehow, every month, you succeed

in company standards and get promoted

employee of the fucking year

eotfy

i wish i weren't a girl

periods of time

i scream for a lifeline

my body is never going to be mine

it's yours for the taking

the men tell me i'm wrong,

but i try to measure my reaction just right

i have always put up a good fight

but not too much

to say no, it has to be calculated

from boys

playing with girls until they're broken toys

i can't afford

another night with makeup covering my wilted eyes

i love being a girl, just not at their expense

girlhood
-july 23rd, 2023

you were inside of Her

you cleansed your body with Her

you gave Her a safe space to rest Her head

you showed Her the grace you had never shown me

you let Her smile and giggle around you

she was filled by you

she lathered Her body with the eucalyptus soap

in the shower that i tirelessly scrubbed on my knees

she laid Her head on my reserved place

on your chest

she felt comfortable enough to show Her sunshine

she got everything i vied for so effortlessly

all for what? dare i ask

you got a good fuck, and i feel empty

Her moans drew you in like a siren

what a pathetic little alcoholic sailor

i will not purify my mind of

your grotesque behavior once more

my homeland was raided once again

so i am waving the white flag this time

all the historical architecture burned to the ground

you can try to rebuild,

but hell has shattered our foundation

burn the sage all around,

but the sacred grounds have spirits roaming

i fear the damage is done

does this fathom a reaction from you

in the slightest?

Her

i'll never be her

so is that why you are happier?

drinking the rum on the beach

when she's down on her knees

tell me, was she better than me?

she's so goddamn tempting

that's precisely why you're going straight to hell

i never did anything to you,

so why am i black and blue?

you beat me down to the floor

you're so goddamn self implored

i don't fucking need this anymore

we both know i can't walk out the door

we are the inside jokes

can't make you happier

'cause you love the dirty girls

you cleaned me up nice

to then throw me into the dirt

that's exactly why you're going straight to hell

i'm ready to die in spite of you

"i fucking hate you," echos through the room

i can't make you any happier

it sent me to spiral swirls

why the fuck did you pretend you were in love?

inside jokes

-november 16th, 2022

we got name tattoos before i ever loved you

on my 20th birthday, i wished for us

two weeks later, there was another one

i know three's a crowd, a shit show party

pushed me the blame for your doing

with her, do you have more fun?

all i did was love you,

so why am i covering bruises?

i feel useless these days

my naked body is an embarrassment to myself

cinderella cried home shoeless

when you took her hand, i was writing you poems

how foolish

clock stoke 12, i am crying in the shower

all i did was love you,

so why am i covering bruises?

you told me i was useless

cinderella cried home shoeless

and you were in the bar dancing

i am so clueless

why can't you hold me a little longer?

my body is for you, so why won't you touch it?

should've known i wasn't the only one

by the first kiss

black and blue teary eyes dedicated to you

thought your jealousy was

just a testament to intense love

when you kicked me down,

how was the view from above?

it was never just us two,

so tell me, to whom did you give the shoe?

cinderella was me, but i didn't know you had her too

i am a beautiful little fool, so, again, i'll ask

all i did was love you,

why am i covering bruises?

cinderella

-november 12th, 2022

how dare there be another

my white blood cells are scathing

the amount of fucking work they put in just for you

to slice at the scar again

i fear i am standing under a cycling blade

that i won't admit to

i fear even my body knows i won't move

and refuses to help

i will just be surprised every time i get cut

the first time was a shock

but i've lost so much blood now,

i point my bloody fingers and refuse to admit blame

my white blood cells are unforgiving

bleeding out

i knew i was fucked in the head with trauma

when i wished on my 20th birthday candles

that you wouldn't hit me anymore

i wish...

-july 26th, 2022

limbs raised,

eyes clenched

i beg for mercy

-may 18th, 2022

down on my knees

repenting for my sins

when i said i liked it rough,

this is not what i meant

oh, dear god

my heavenly body grazed your caramel skin

every time you pulled me in

your embrace feels rewarding

if my skin's painted purple and blue by your power,

hopefully, then you'll truly see how delicate i am

a divine being weeping over lucifer

how insufferable is that?

swollen teary eyes and puffy lips

pouting out for you

kiss me, please, i need your hands on my skin

take my breath, mouth fuck me

no matter if it's pain or pleasure

i tend to confuse the two for love

forever mistaking your silhouette

as the heavens opening above

passion or death

take my breath, mouth fuck me

screaming, "shut up"

mouth fucked

i have a burning desire

to be forgotten by you

i've had enough for a lifetime

said you needed space, so i

gathered the stars for your orbit

i selected them carefully for hours, hoping that

when i revealed them to you,

you'd feel relief

you threw them down and said,

"shut up and stop crying,

your loves a fucking disease

so damn needy

you do nothing but sit around and weep,"

so i embraced the bed, made good on your word,

and cried myself to sleep

hush, little baby

i know you're a hard one to please

looked for your approval in everything

so when you kick me down, i will fall gracefully

and look up to you, wondering if i did so correctly

please say, 'hush, little baby,'

looking up to the sky,

begging the moon for another chance

kissing the night goodbye

as i sing the stars my lullabies,

i explained i needed to leave

i want to feel relief for once

the way i try so hard to make you feel

shut up

so there i am, lying to my therapist!

sitting in this tiny room

listening to the fluorescent lights' slight buzz

talking about grieving a relationship i'm still in

i'm bracing for a crash before i even get in the car

my driving will not improve

even if i know what's to come

preparing myself like a soldier whose mission

will be to die on this battlefield

pretending you lost someone you're still with

feels just as deadly

and comical is a sadistic way

so the punchline goes…

i know i will feel this pain twice

…and get this! you won't believe it,

i got a two-for-one in trauma!

lying to my therapist

we won't be together

maybe in the next life

he hits me so hard

i'm flinching my eyes so tight

but he'll cry he's sorry later

and i know i'll still kiss him goodnight

"i promise i'll never do it again"
-august 29th, 2022

my laughter is a protest

to everything you've done to me

rare

woke me up in the middle of the night to show

we are electrical beings

static electricity blew fireworks in your mind

where did our lightning go?

the polarity in our magnetic field is irreversible

it's not magic, it's the truth

"wake up, look at this"

-november 16th, 2022

you brought a new meaning
of a wide-eyed gaze to life for me
made me experience aesthetic things
you knew i'd fall for your lackluster lies
and turn them into post-midnight cries
then project everything into my poetry

muse
-august 7th, 2023

don't let me go even if i scream to go away

please, even if i make it hard to stay

hard to love

-october 16th, 2022

"why does she stay?"

well, long story short,

i don't know

i trauma bonded

in all the violence that surrounded him,

there was safety from myself

even in the worst moments of my life,

he was with me for it

he knew what it was like in the hotel room

he knew my heart was breaking in the clinic

he watched as i lost my mind in the hospital

he was there when i got the news that

my heart in human form went to heaven

he witnessed his infidelity firsthand

he only knows what i'm like in pure survival mode

when someone is beating me senseless

although he caused the turbulence,

only he was there to watch me suffer

there is no greater understanding

than the person who caused the pain

at the end of the day,

he brought me flowers

he carved our initials into a tree

he sat with me as doctors were in and out

he bought me paper lanterns to fly into the moon

the traumas of the last two years,

we witnessed together

i don't have the strength,

but i do have a passion for him

why i stay

violence

love

ariel was my first crush

longing for love

watching the water glimmer, looking up

cherry locks and a voice like honey

she never broke my heart

years later, the first man i loved

left me on curbsides, clothes packed

unstable anger, cuban link chains, and beer breath

all the empty promises with nothing to show

hard to think he was my father

watched a dear friend fall for his first love

puppy love, high school sweethearts, skipping beats

fairytale wedding, spinning in her heels

it all came crashing down like fine china

infidelity and kitchen table bills

took him for granted, and he chose himself

now, he spends nights racking up beer cans

wondering if he could've been more of a better man

the girl next door came dancing into my life

golden hair, elvira replica, sniffing her magic away

the most ethereal girl i have ever laid my eyes on

sunshine in her smile, moonlight in her eyes

twin flame, she proved it was real

she passed years later, and now i lay

every night, the moon watches my eyes rain

here came the boy to show me fun

the love under my heart this time

he showed me pain, took my angel away

black eyes, scared nights, illicit affair lies

who knew at 20, i could feel my hope die

this is the story of love

no matter how much i scream

"enough is enough."

all the hearts keep breaking

puppy love to the dog days

we spoke of our deepest secrets all night

and by the end, i even let you see my birthmark

intimate

-may 23rd, 2022

fill your fingers in my body

am i warm?

how sweet does it taste?

sorry, i don't know heaven

time to eat, heads down, say grace

nectarine

-september 23, 2021

love

your

       beauty

          puts

              the bromeliads to shame

incomparable

birthday cake is better at midnight

and i love you feels better when you're not

expecting to hear it

cherry on top

-august 29rd, 2022

singing you sonnets

'til my face turns blue

the blues

-august 4th, 2022

soft-spoken with butterfly wings

24k golden hair, peach glossed lips

tattoos of a dragon and a rose

angel kisses across your nose

lovely lullaby baby

dirty toys in the back of your closet

height measured on a wall

my tiny girl, 5'2" tall

we were living a natural high

playing house, staying awake all night

the love in the movies was real

laying on blankets under the stars

cherry ice pops, singing all night long

we were so madly in love with each other

had a marvelous time giving you everything

thank you for dancing in and changing my life

forever

emily

the way your blonde hair grazes your shoulders

baby yellow crop top and belly rings uniform

5'2", gassing it in your blue chevy

you'd sit in front of your reflection

and put on 10 coats of mascara for an hour

i'd lie and tell you they didn't look clumpy

the way you'd carry around the same wilted stuffed

animal koala since you were 6

the way you could make me laugh until my ribs hurt

you were the only person who could make me

cry of happiness

why'd you have to keep chasing a high?

this life with you was my high

my high

spanish moss danced in your wise oaks,

and we fed it to the palominos

we were too busy in love to notice anything else

but our fairy tale

summer days with you

-december 26th, 2023

loving is the scariest feeling

in the whole wide world

terrified

-july 7th, 2022

the sound of horses trotting will shake me up like

never imagined

rupturing every bone in my body

my skin vibrates, goosebumps come forth

my knees were weak, ready to drop

i said goodbye to that dirt rollercoaster

of a driveway

i realized i could never lay in this yard

and have this view of the stars anymore

a tear falls while watching what was once our home

in the rearview mirror

please, please, please, get sober

last call

-june 1st 2021

you will never be unloved by me

you are too well entangled in my soul

knots

-june 22nd, 2022

the universe breathed a sigh of relief

when our bodies connected again

i missed you

-may 20th, 2021

you make me feel older than 17

taking care of you keeps me sane

then you died

now i

can't imagine turning 25

can't fathom being alive

aging out

-may 16th, 2021

if you were still alive,

i know you would have heard about the cicadas

i know fear would have waltzed through your mind

 like an 1800s ball

i know i would have held you and told you they

weren't near

i would've let them eat me whole

before ever touching you

i took the blessing of protecting you for granted

so i will wait and listen to them

sing at sunset in the meantime

in my head, it's your lilac love sent

from the heavens above

bug

love

is

only

but

a

metaphor

for

god

i found god once

i think i'm way too young

and clouded with my vices for love,

and i think he's the same

first impression
-january 1st, 2022

with eyes that could kill,

wipe the mascara dripping down her cheeks

tear the clothes off her body

wrapped up around you

the choking, the suffocating

gasping as you are rock-hard

bruised knees and sore throat

opened wide, warm, and wet

ready to swallow you whole

medusa

love

setting clocks through my sleep

just case you sent that 3am text

desperate

i will write your last name next to my name in
pretty pretty cursive a million times over on paper

crush

fantasy on the side

another option for when you're bored

twisted my morals to the core

better to be loved second than not at all

booty call

love

-and just like that,

the 3 am phone call made me fall all over again

still desperate

kiss and tell,

but i'm the little secret

even if the right side of my bed

smells like you

love is embarrassing

i'll change who i am

to keep holding your hand

pathetic

mimosas and lobster brunch

a good afternoon

but i am a liability, i'll fuck it up soon

i picked out your favorite perfume

to wear when we go to the cinema

then i spilled my popcorn

god, i'm such a fuck up

liability

love

sweet tea with lemon please

hints of sour mixed with sugar are my specialty

no wonder i love you so dearly

sweet n' sour

i showed you

vanilla ice cream with warm apple pie

you showed me

bottle service and pretty night lights

i showed you

the scars on my thighs

you showed me

how to look into people's eyes

out of my shell

tickets for two, popcorn butter on the bottom

tan skin and brown eyes, this time i gottem

live music, dinner margaritas, we're laughing

for once, everything's okay

this is the calm in the storm

date night

love

i guess if i'm forced to be here and endure,

i might as well love myself

make the best of it

we are the universe

and the universe wanted so desperately to

experience itself

how breathtaking is that?

we fall in love with each other

therefore, the universe falls in love

with itself every day

who are we to be mean to the universe

this is us

if we can fall so profoundly in love with someone

how are we not to fall so deeply in love

with ourselves?

universal love

i guess when all is said and done,

i manifested my own demise

learn from this poetry

do not internalize my words

i am nothing more than a woman who

romanticizes pain

and works it out in therapy

holding my dead flowers,

screaming my pretty words

sugar is heated to caramel for one to eat

poets are a walking form of turmoil and catastrophe

trying to make sense of pain through a page

bled with ink

the caramelized butterflies

thank you for reaching the end before i met mine

*of all the things i've done in my life, i can say this is
my proudest moment*

*a spiritual reader once told me i would do
something with my shit end of the stick, i'm betting
this is what she meant*

-

*the trigger warnings of caramelized butterflies is a
collection of poetry containing my triggers*

*growing up, addiction, hating myself, struggling
with borderline personality, ptsd and understanding
love*

*it's not meant to be hopeful and uprising, it was
meant to tell my ugly truth*

spilling my guts

-

*pure, innocent, raw sugar is heated to hell to make
caramel for others to consume and enjoy*

i have yet to cool down and share coping skills

so, for now, this is

the trigger warnings of caramelized butterflies

the trigger warnings of

caramelized butterflies

ayanna jade luevano

Printed in the USA
CPSIA information can be obtained
at www.ICGtesting.com
LVHW010828080924
790209LV00016B/965